A GIRL JUST LIKE ME

WRITTEN BY PEARL VALCIN

THIS BOOK BELONGS TO:

This book is dedicated to my beautiful niece Darliya. I want to remind you that you are unique and that you are filled with greatness. The sky is the limit, and that you can do whatever you put your mind to.

A girl just like me, helped pave the way.
A girl just like me helped save the day.

A girl like me stands tall.
A girl like me can do it all.

A girl like Harriet Tubman helped free the slaves.
Just like Harriet, I am not afraid.

I can be courageous like Angela Davis,
standing up for what is right.

A girl like me always shines bright!

I can become a boxer like Laila Ali.
Winning championships as strong as I can be.

I can knock down barriers like Dr. Rebecca Lee Kepler, becoming an author and a doctor, making my own way.

I can pass the bar and become a lawyer like
Charlotte E Ray.
A girl like me shines all day!

As long as I work hard, nothing will ever stand in my way!

I can reach for the stars, Venus, Pluto, even Mars!

I can become an astronaut like Mae C. Jemison, traveling into space.

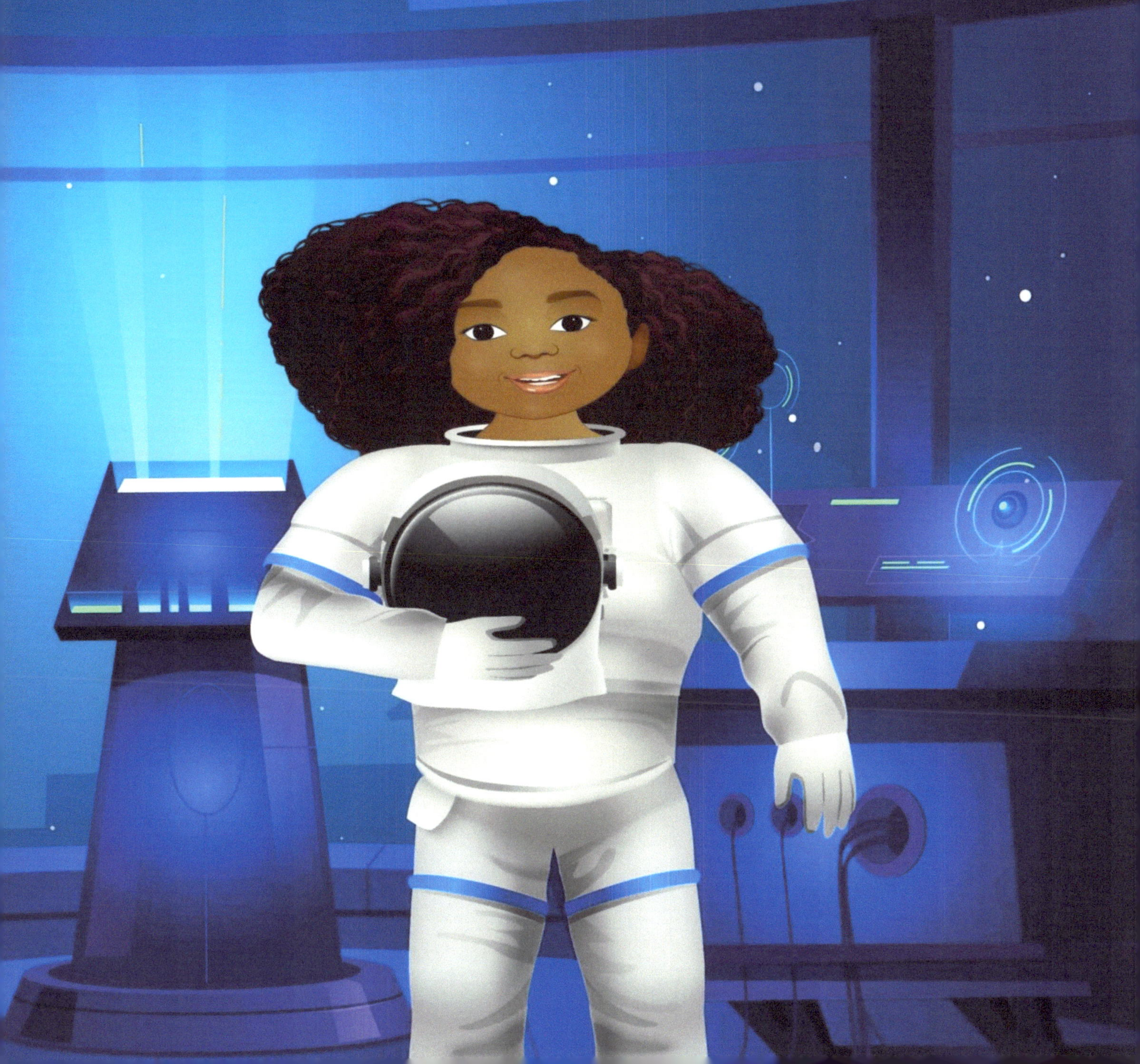

I can even become a pilot like Bessie Coleman,
flying from place to place.

The sky is the limit. There is nothing that I cannot achieve. All I have to do is believe.

I can change the world. I am filled with strength and grace. I can make the world a better place.

A girl like me so talented and true.
I can do whatever I put my mind to.

**A girl like me is capable of extraordinary things.
Just like my ancestors I can do anything!**

Fun Facts

Harriet Tubman

Harriet Tubman escaped slavery and helped conduct the underground railroad. She helped rescue and free over 70 salves.

Laila Ali

Laila Ali fought as a professional boxer from 1999 to 2007, she retired winning 24 championships, and zero losses.

Charlotte E. Ray

Charlotte E. Ray was the first African American female to become a lawyer in the United States. She graduated from Howard University February 27, 1827 becoming the first woman to complete her law degree from Howard University of Law.

Mae Carol Jemison

On June 4, 1987 Mae Carol Jemison was the first African American woman to be admitted into NASA's training program. September 12, 1992 she was also the first African American woman to fly into space.

Fun Facts

Bessie Coleman

Bessie Coleman was the first African American woman to receive her pilot license. June 15th, 1921 she was also the first African American to receive her international pilot license.

Dr. Rebecca Lee Crumpler

In 1864 Dr. Rebecca Lee Crumpler was the first African American woman to become a doctor in the United States. She was also one of the first female physician authors in the U.S.

Angela Davis

Angela Davis was born January 26, 1944. She is known for being a political activist, philosopher, educator, and author. On May 1, 1979 she was awarded the Lenin Peace Prize from the Soviet Union.

www.ingramcontent.com/pod-product-compliance
Ingram Content Group UK Ltd.
Pitfield, Milton Keynes, MK11 3LW, UK
UKHW061030310726
14089UKWH00009B/182
* 9 7 8 1 7 3 7 3 0 2 6 4 3 *